A Letter from Your Teacher

On the first day of School

written by
Shannon Olsen

Illustrated by
Sandie Sonke

2021 Orange County, California

ISBN Numbers 978-1-7354141-2-6 (paperback) 978-1-7354141-3-3 (hardcover)

Library of Congress Control Number: 2021906911

For all of "my kids."
I'm so lucky to have been your teacher. - S.O.

For Geniece, Brian, Dash and Arrow - S.S.

Dear Student,

This is a little welcome note
I want to share with you.
Believe all that I'm about to say,
because every word is true.

There are a few important things
I'd like for you to know.
All throughout the school year,
our relationship will grow.

I cannot wait to get to know you and all the things that make you YOU.

Do you play sports or like to draw?

Maybe you even do kung fu!

I'll get to meet your family,

and hear the places you have been.

I want to know
your favorite subject,

and see awards that
you may win.

I promise every morning
to greet you with a smile.
We'll give high-fives and hugs
or fist bump, if that's your style!

I will celebrate with you
when you have exciting news

like, "It's my dog's birthday!"

or, "I got brand new shoes!"

I'm here so you can learn
a lot of science, math, and reading.

I'll help you with your writing
and all the skills you will be needing.

But learning is not just about
the schoolwork that we do.

Some values that I hope you'll gain
are empathy and kindness too.

You can also be respectful
by listening with your ears and eyes.

Read pages
10 – 15
Reader's Notebook

Follow directions the first time
and take good care of your supplies!

CRAYONS

I want you to set high goals
and persevere through any test.

When it comes to working hard,
I expect you'll try your very best.

Some days will be a challenge.
You may think, "I just can't do it."

Even when you cannot YET,
I am here to help you through it!

I'm going to try to make you laugh
and put a smile on your face.

AMAZiNG THiNGS HAPPEN HERE!

We will make learning
lots of fun.
This is our happy place!

I'm excited that you're here!
Day by day, I hope you'll see
I love being your teacher
and you mean so much to me.

Love,

_____

A Letter from the Author

Dear Teacher,

This book is meant to be a letter from you, but I also wanted to take a moment to write a letter TO you.

I know you have a huge heart. It's sort of a given in order to be in this profession. As a fellow educator who has spent much time in the classroom, I know that you pour a great deal of blood, sweat, and tears into your job. You not only work hard to teach academic skills (and to balance all of the extra responsibilities on top of that), but you dedicate yourself to building connections with kids.

It can be hard to put into words how much you care for your students. You show it through various "love languages." Teachers give words of affirmation, physical gestures such as high-fives and hugs (and fist bumps), quality time, acts of service, and even gifts. At one time or another, you've probably spent your Sunday night assembling Valentines or little treat bags.

But one of your most powerful love languages as a teacher is reading aloud to students. It has always been (and always will be) a magical way to communicate information to kids. When you introduce any new concept or topic, it's likely that you might read aloud a book to get your students excited and thinking about it.

And on the first day of school, there are so many of those new things that you want to share. It is your first chance to set the tone for the class and for the rest of the year. There are all of the rules and procedures of course, but Day 1 is also the foundation for building relationships. I know that it's important to you to begin making positive connections with your students right out the gate, so I wanted to create a picture book that could help with that.

I wrote *Our Class is a Family* in the hopes that it would encourage class community and help students feel a sense of belonging at school. The book focuses on peer relationships in the classroom, but it also mentions the role of the teacher in a class family. One of the lines is, "Your teacher is here for you." In *A Letter From Your Teacher*, I wanted to expand upon this statement and help kids to further understand what that really means.

This book is a sort of universal letter that could be read aloud by any teacher. But I invite you to sign your own name on the last page, as a message to your students that the letter is coming straight from you.

Every class family is special and unique of course, and I'm sure there are many more things you would include in a more personal letter to your own students. Maybe you love when they invite you to their sporting events or recitals, or maybe you want to share what you have in common with them, such as a love of movies or having pets at home. I hope that this book can be used as a jumping off point for sharing all of those details that make you YOU.

Thank you for all that you do for your kids. You mean so much to them!

With love,

About the Author

Shannon Olsen has taught second grade for fifteen years. She is from Southern California and obtained her B.A. in English and M.A. in Teaching from University of California, Irvine. Shannon loves traveling and spending time with her husband and two daughters. Visit www.lifebetweensummers.com for her teacher resources, book companions, and information about author visits.

About the Illustrator

Sandie Sonke is also a Southern California native with a degree in studio art from California State University Fullerton. She is a fan of coffee and cooking, and among the many hats she wears, her favorite role is being a mom of two. Sandie has published several children's books, and you can also find more of her freelance illustration work at www.sandiesonkeillustration.com.

Made in the USA
Coppell, TX
13 August 2021

60443747R00019